Cool STUFF for

— for —

BATH & BEAUTY

A Division of ABDO
ABDO
Publishing Company

PAM SCHEUNEMANN

visit us at www.abdopublishing.com

Published by ABDO Publishing Company, a division of ABDO, P.O. Box 398166, Minneapolis, Minnesota 55439. Copyright © 2012 by Abdo Consulting Group, Inc. International copyrights reserved in all countries. No part of this book may be reproduced in any form without written permission from the publisher. Checkerboard Library™ is a trademark and logo of ABDO Publishing Company.

Printed in the United States of America, North Mankato, Minnesota
052011
092011

PRINTED ON RECYCLED PAPER

Design and Production: Mighty Media, Inc.
Series Editors: Katherine Hengel and Liz Salzmann
Photo Credits: Anders Hanson, Shutterstock

The following manufacturers/names appearing in this book are trademarks:
Alaffia® Sustainable Skin Care™, Anchor®, Argo®, Arm & Hammer®, Aura Cacia®, Avery®, Crafter's Pick™, Desert Essence®, Equate®, Gulf Wax®, Palmer's®, Pyrex®, Spectrum®, Wilton®, Wilton® Candy Melts®

Library of Congress Cataloging-in-Publication Data
Scheunemann, Pam, 1955-
  Cool stuff for bath & beauty : creative handmade projects for kids / Pam Scheunemann.
    p. cm. -- (Cool stuff)
  Includes index.
  ISBN 978-1-61714-980-1
  1. Hygiene products--Juvenile literature. 2. Creative activities and seat work--Juvenile literature. I. Title. II. Title: Cool stuff for bath and beauty.
  RA778.5.S34 2012
  613'.4--dc22
                          2011003049

CONTENTS

BEAUTY

It's no secret that people have been using beauty products for thousands of years. Throughout history every possible ingredient has been used. Beauty products have been made out of everything from avocados to animal fat. Some of these products were even found to be harmful. Today all products for the body are tested for safety.

In this book you'll find recipes to make some of your own beauty products. There are also activities to make some cool beauty stuff too! These are things you can make for yourself or for someone else. These projects use safe ingredients that are easy to find.

Permission & Safety

- Always get **permission** before making any type of craft at home.

- Ask if you can use the tools and ingredients needed.

- If you'd like to do something by yourself, say so. Just make sure you do it safely.

- Ask for help when necessary.

- Be careful when using knives, scissors, or other sharp objects.

- Only use the oven or microwave when an adult is around.

- If you need to touch something hot, use oven mitts, not **towels**!

Be Prepared

- Read the entire activity before you begin.

- Make sure you have all the tools and **materials** listed.

- Do you have enough time to complete the project?

- Keep your work area clean and organized.

- Follow the directions for each activity.

- Clean up after you are finished for the day.

TOOLS AND

BAKING SODA

CITRIC ACID POWDER

CORNSTARCH

COCONUT OIL

FOOD COLORING

OIL-BASED
CANDY FLAVORING

SHEA BUTTER

22-GAUGE WIRE

NEEDLE-NOSE
PLIERS

WIRE CUTTERS

SEED BEADS

CENTER BEADS

MATERIALS

PETROLEUM JELLY

CANDY MELT

BEESWAX

GRATED PARAFFIN WAX

BUTTON COVER KIT

SOAP MOLDS

CRAFT STICK

FABRIC GLUE

SMALL CONTAINERS

COCOA BUTTER

3-DRAWER ORGANIZER

WITCH HAZEL

ESSENTIAL OILS

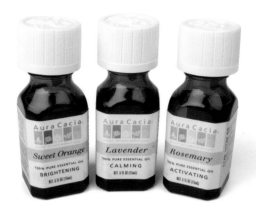

Essential oils are made from plants. By using different methods, the perfume of the plant is collected. Only a few drops are needed since the scent is so **concentrated**. Most essential oils are too strong to use directly on the skin. Carrier oils are used to **dilute** the essential oil. Both of these types of oils may be found at natural food stores.

CARRIER OILS

Carrier oils are usually vegetable oils. The different types of carrier oils are for different purposes. Sweet almond oil is good for smoothing the skin. Jojoba oil is very close to the skin's natural oils. Cocoa butter and shea butter are solid at room temperature. This makes them good carrier oils for **lotions** and creams.

BATH SALTS

Bath salts have been used for their health benefits for centuries. There are many different kinds of salt. Different salts **contain** different minerals that are good for the body. Some salts are coarse and some are fine.

Each type of salt has its own uses and benefits. For example, using Dead Sea bath salt is said to be good for dry skin. Himalayan Pink salt is thought to soothe sore muscles.

Epsom salt has many health benefits, but it isn't salt! It is actually another mineral. It is great for softening the skin.

DEAD SEA SALT

HIMALAYAN PINK SALT

EPSOM SALT

SEA SALT

Allergy Alert

Some people may be **allergic** to some of the ingredients used in these activities. Be sure to let people know what's in any product you give as a gift. Always try the product on a small area of skin. That way you can see if you have any allergies or bad reactions. If so, don't use the product to cover a large area of skin. Wash it off immediately with soap and water.

Luscious
LIP GLOSS

TRY SMACKING YOUR LIPS WITH THIS!

STUFF YOU'LL NEED

1/4 TEASPOON GRATED PARAFFIN WAX

1 TEASPOON COCONUT OIL

1 TEASPOON PETROLEUM JELLY

1 WILTON CANDY MELT

1/8 TEASPOON OIL-BASED CANDY FLAVORING

RESEALABLE PLASTIC BAG

MEASURING SPOONS

BOWL OF WATER

OVEN MITTS

SCISSORS

SMALL CONTAINER

1 Put all of the ingredients into the plastic bag. Seal the bag.

2 Heat the bowl of water in the microwave. Use oven mitts to remove the hot bowl.

3 Place the sealed bag in the hot water until the ingredients melt.

4 Take the bag out of the water. Knead the bag with your fingers until the ingredients are mixed together. This must be done before the mixture hardens.

5 Cut off the tip of a corner of the bag. Squeeze the lip gloss into a clean **container**. Place it in the refrigerator to cool.

TIPS

- *Make your own labels. You could have a label for each different flavor!*

- *Double the recipe to make more of one flavor.*

Smoothing
SALT SCRUB

STUFF YOU'LL NEED

4 OUNCES JOJOBA OIL
3-5 DROPS ESSENTIAL OIL
1 CUP FINE SEA SALT
FOOD COLORING (OPTIONAL)

MIXING BOWL
MEASURING CUP
SPOON
STORAGE JAR

*Salt **scrubs** are made of oil, salt, and **fragrance**. There are many kinds of each of these ingredients.*

1. Put the oils and sea salt in a mixing bowl.

2. Add a few drops of food coloring if you'd like to color your salt scrub.

3. Mix thoroughly.

4. Put the mixture in a storage jar.

5. To use, stir the scrub and then take a bit out of the jar. Scrub your skin with it. Rinse it off.

TIP

The oil may separate from the salt. Stir the mixture before using.

13

Delightful
BATH SALTS

SOAK IN HEAVENLY LUXURY!

14

STUFF YOU'LL NEED

2 CUPS BATH SALT
2-5 DROPS ESSENTIAL OIL
1-2 DROPS FOOD COLORING
MIXING BOWL

MEASURING CUP
SPOON
STORAGE JAR
RIBBON

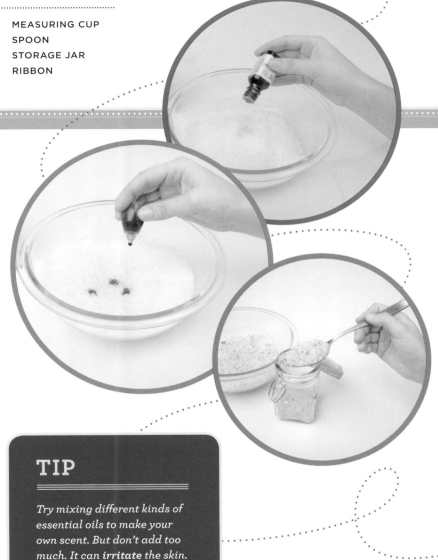

1 Put the salt in a bowl.

2 Add the essential oil and mix thoroughly.

3 Add the food coloring and mix thoroughly.

4 Put the mixture in a storage jar.

5 Decorate the jar with a ribbon for yourself or to give as a gift!

6 To use, put a cup of bath salt in a hot bath. Enjoy!

You can recycle glass jars with lids. Wash them thoroughly, remove labels, and decorate the lid!

TIP

*Try mixing different kinds of essential oils to make your own scent. But don't add too much. It can **irritate** the skin.*

Bath
BUBBLERS

PUT SOME PIZZAZZ IN YOUR BATH!

STUFF YOU'LL NEED

1/2 CUP CORNSTARCH
1/2 CUP CITRIC ACID POWDER
1 CUP BAKING SODA
SPOON
1 TABLESPOON SWEET ALMOND OIL

3-5 DROPS ESSENTIAL OIL
WITCH HAZEL
FOOD COLORING (OPTIONAL)
LARGE GLASS MIXING BOWLS
SMALL SPRAY BOTTLE

RUBBER GLOVES
DOME SOAP MOLD
WAX PAPER

1. Put the dry ingredients in a large glass bowl. Mix thoroughly.

2. Add the sweet almond oil and essential oil. Mix thoroughly.

3. Put the witch hazel in the spray bottle. If desired, add 3 or 4 drops of food coloring to the witch hazel.

4. Put on the rubber gloves. Spray the dry mixture three times with the witch hazel. Then use your hands to mix it thoroughly.

5. Repeat step four 7 to 9 times. Be careful! Too much liquid can cause the fizzing to begin! The mixture should feel like damp sand, but not too wet. Squeeze some of it in your hand. If it forms a clump, it is ready for the mold.

6. Pack some of the mixture in each half of the dome mold. Overfill it a little. Press the halves together to form a good ball; Slide a bit while pressing, but do not twist!

7. Gently pinch the mold to remove the ball. Set it on wax paper to dry.

8. To use, just drop one into your bath.

TIP

Try using fun-shaped ice cube trays or candy molds instead of the dome molds.

Mellow
BATH MELTS

THIS SKIN-SOFTENING BATH MELT IS SURE TO BE A HIT!

STUFF YOU'LL NEED

2 CUPS COCOA BUTTER
TABLESPOON
2 TABLESPOONS SWEET ALMOND OIL
10-20 DROPS ESSENTIAL OIL

GLASS MEASURING CUP
FRYING PAN
OVEN MITT
CRAFT STICK OR WOODEN SKEWER

SOAP OR CANDY MOLDS
COOKIE SHEET
FOIL OR TISSUE PAPER

1   Put the cocoa butter in the glass measuring cup.

2   Put 1 inch of water in the frying pan. Place the measuring cup in the pan. Put it on the stove with the burner on low.

3   Stir the cocoa butter with a craft stick or wooden skewer until it is just melted.

4   Add the sweet almond oil. Stir. Turn off the stove. Using an oven mitt, lift the measuring cup and place it on the counter.

5   Let the mixture cool for 3 minutes. Then add the essential oil and mix.

6   Set the molds on a cookie sheet. Pour the mixture into the molds. Put the filled molds into the freezer for

15 to 20 minutes, just until the melts become solid. Don't let them freeze. If they freeze, the melts could crack.

7   Pop the melts out of the molds. Wrap them in foil or tissue paper. Store them in a cool place.

8   To use, drop one or two melts into your bathtub and get **mellow**!

TIP

These melts will leave your tub very slippery. Be very careful when getting in and out of the bath.

Handy
HAND LOTION

20

STUFF YOU'LL NEED

4 OUNCES SHEA BUTTER
4 OUNCES BEESWAX
5 OUNCES JOJOBA OIL
TEASPOON

2 TEASPOONS ESSENTIAL OIL
2 GLASS MEASURING CUPS
FRYING PAN
OVEN MITT

CRAFT STICK OR WOODEN SKEWER
SOAP OR CANDY MOLDS
COOKIE SHEET
FOIL OR PLASTIC BAGS

1   Put the shea butter in a glass measuring cup.

2   Put the beeswax and jojoba oil into the second glass measuring cup.

3   Put 1 inch of water in the frying pan. Place the glass measuring cups in the pan. Put it on the stove with the burner on low.

4   Stir both measuring cups with a craft stick or wooden skewer until the ingredients are just melted.

5   When ingredients are both melted, mix them together. Turn off the stove. Using an oven mitt, lift the measuring cup and place it on the counter.

6   Let the mixture cool for about 3 minutes.

7   Add the essential oil and mix.

8   Set the molds on a cookie sheet. Pour the mixture into the molds. Wait about 1 to 2 hours for it to harden.

9   Pop the bars out of the mold. Wrap them in foil or plastic bags. Store them in a cool place.

10   To use, rub a **lotion** bar with your hands. The heat from your skin will melt enough of the lotion to soften your hands!

MAKEUP BOX

CLEAR THE CLUTTER WITH THIS CUTE STORAGE BOX!

nail polish

lipgloss

hair ties

STUFF YOU'LL NEED

SMALL 3-DRAWER ORGANIZER
RULER
DECORATIVE PAPER
SCISSORS

TAPE
STICKY LABELS
MARKERS
STICKERS

DECORATIVE GEMS
GLUE

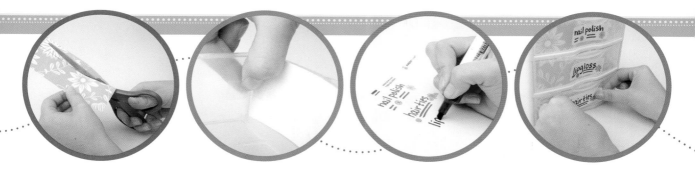

1   Use the ruler to measure the inside of the fronts of the drawers.

2   Draw the **measurements** on the decorative paper. Cut out the shapes.

3   Place the decorative paper shapes inside the drawer fronts. Tape the edges of the paper to the sides of the drawers. This will hold the paper in place without the tape showing.

4   Make a label for each drawer. Use markers, stickers, or your computer to **design** the labels.

5   Put the labels on the drawers. Glue gems to the front of each drawer for decoration.

MATCHING BRUSH HOLDER

Make a brush holder out of a small clear vase or jar. Cut a piece of the decorative paper to line the jar. Add uncooked rice or dried beans. Add your brushes!

It's a Wrap!
HEADBAND

STUFF YOU'LL NEED

COATED PLASTIC HEADBAND
RIBBON
SCISSORS
FABRIC GLUE

1   Cut a piece of ribbon three times longer than the headband.

2   Place the end of the ribbon on the inside of one end of the headband. Use a dab of glue to hold it in place. Let it dry a few minutes.

3   Start by wrapping the ribbon once around the end of the headband. Then angle the ribbon and continue wrapping.

4   Keep wrapping the ribbon around the headband. You can leave gaps or cover the headband completely.

5   When you reach the end, wrap the ribbon once more around the end and glue it in place. Let it dry.

6   Cut off any extra ribbon.

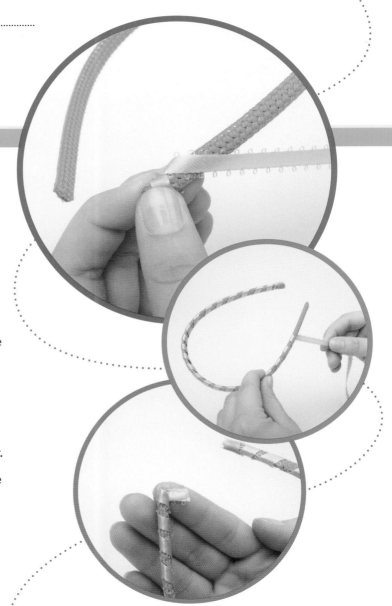

Brilliant Button
PONYTAIL TIES

THESE ARE QUICK AND EASY TO MAKE!

STUFF YOU'LL NEED

BUTTON COVER KIT
NEEDLE-NOSE PLIERS
WIRE CUTTERS

RULER
22-GAUGE WIRE
PONYTAIL HOLDER

FABRIC
SCISSORS

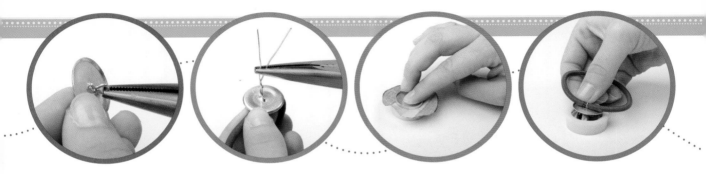

1. Use the needle-nose pliers to remove the loop from the button back.

2. Use the wire cutters to cut a piece of wire about 3 inches (8 cm) long. Bend the wire in half.

3. Put the ponytail holder in the bend of the wire. Hold the button back with the bent edge facing up. Stick the ends of the wire down through the holes on the button back.

4. Use the needle-nose pliers to twist the ends of the wire together until the ponytail holder is snug against the button back. Be careful not to twist the wire too hard.

5. Cut the wire ends so they are about ½ inch (1.25 cm) long. Bend them so they rest flat against the button back.

6. Cut a piece of fabric using the pattern that came with the button kit.

7. Place the fabric and button cover on the rubber holder from the button kit. Snap it into place, folding the fabric over.

8. Place the button back on the button cover and snap into place using your fingers.

9. Remove the button from the rubber holder.

Beaded Flower
HAIRPINS

STUFF YOU'LL NEED

22-GAUGE WIRE
SEED BEADS
CENTER BEAD

WIRE CUTTERS
BOBBY PINS OR HAIRPINS

1   Pull about 15 inches (38 cm) of wire from the spool. Do not cut!

2   Decide how many petals you'd like your flower to have. Count out 15 seed beads for each petal. For example, five petals takes 75 seed beads.

3   Put the center bead on the wire. Then add all the seed beads. Twist a small loop at the end of the wire.

4   Push the beads toward the spool. Then slide 15 beads (enough for one petal) back to about 5 inches (13 cm) from the end of the wire. To make the first petal form a loop with the beads and twist it twice to secure the beads.

5   Slide the beads for the second petal down to where the first petal was formed. Form a loop with the beads and twist it twice. Bring the spool end of the wire up next to the new petal. Repeat this step for the rest of your petals.

6   Push the center bead to the middle of the flower and wrap the spool end of the wire to the back of the flower. Twist the ends of wire tightly together against the back.

7   Straighten the ends. Cut the wire from the spool even with the tail end.

8   Wrap the ends of the wire tightly around the bobby pin or hairpin. Trim any extra wire.

CONCLUSION

It's important to take good care of your skin. Do some **research** on different bath and beauty products. Make and try out some of the projects in this book. You'll be amazed at the beauty products you can make out of things in your kitchen!

Go a step further. Take some time to learn about **aromatherapy.** Try different scents. It's fun to learn about the different properties of essential oils. You can mix your own combinations.

Don't spend a fortune on bath products. Make your own! Be creative with your packaging. These things make great gifts! People love to **pamper** themselves. The sky is the limit!

GLOSSARY

allergic – having an unpleasant reaction after eating, touching, or breathing something.

aromatherapy – the use of different scents to help someone feel better.

concentrate – to make a liquid stronger and thicker by removing water or another liquid from it.

contain – to consist of or include. A *container* is something that other things can be put into.

design – to plan how something will appear or work.

dilute – to make a liquid thinner or weaker by adding water or another liquid.

fragrance – a sweet or pleasant scent.

irritate – to make sore or painful.

lotion – a thin cream that is rubbed into the skin.

material – something that other things can be made of, such as fabric, plastic, or metal.

measurement – a piece of information found by measuring.

mellow – calm and relaxed.

pamper – to give special treatment or care to yourself or someone else.

permission – when a person in charge says it's okay to do something.

research – the act of finding out more about something.

scrub – 1. a rough cleaner used to soften the skin. 2. to clean by rubbing hard.

towel – a cloth or paper used for cleaning or drying.

Web Sites

To learn more about cool stuff, visit ABDO Publishing Company on the World Wide Web at www.abdopublishing.com. Web sites about cool stuff are featured on our Book Links page. These links are routinely monitored and updated to provide the most current information available.